YOUR KNOWLEDGE HAS VALUE

Bibliographic information published by the German National Library:

The German National Library lists this publication in the National Bibliography; detailed bibliographic data are available on the Internet at http://dnb.dnb.de .

Imprint:

Copyright © 2015 GRIN Verlag, Open Publishing GmbH
Print and binding: Books on Demand GmbH, Norderstedt Germany
ISBN: 9783668225930

This book at GRIN:

http://www.grin.com/en/e-book/323354/creation-of-shareholder-value-in-the-pfizer-astrazeneca-deal

Markus Bäder

Aus der Reihe: e-fellows.net stipendiaten-wissen

e-fellows.net (Hrsg.)

Band 1818

Creation of Shareholder Value in the Pfizer-AstraZeneca Deal

GRIN Publishing

GRIN - Your knowledge has value

Since its foundation in 1998, GRIN has specialized in publishing academic texts by students, college teachers and other academics as e-book and printed book. The website www.grin.com is an ideal platform for presenting term papers, final papers, scientific essays, dissertations and specialist books.

Visit us on the internet:

http://www.grin.com/

http://www.facebook.com/grincom

http://www.twitter.com/grin_com

Academic Essay

'Creation of Shareholder Value in the Pfizer-AstraZeneca Deal'

Northumbria University
Academic Year 2014/2015

submitted on 11 May 2015

Table of Contents

List of Figures and Tables

List of Abbreviations

DCF   Discounted Cash Flow Method

EMH   Efficient Market Hypothesis

FCF   Free Cash Flow Model (Capital Structure Theory)

FDI   Foreign Direct Investment

IPO   Initial Public Offering

IRR   Internal Rate of Return

M&A   Merger & Acquisition

M&As   Mergers & Acquisitions

NAV   Net-Asset Valuation Approaches

PER   Price-Earnings Ratio Model

POT   Pecking Order Theory (Capital Structure Theory)

SME   Small and Medium Sized Enterprise

WACC   Weighted Average Costs of Capital

Academic Essay

Creation of Shareholder Value in the Pfizer-AstraZeneca Deal

The pharmaceutical sector has experienced a year of heavy consolidations, with a record breaking M&A volume of $250bn in 2014 (Ward, 2014a). From a shareholder perspective this should, however, cause serious concern as the deals very rarely maximise the owner's wealth. An illustration of this is the failed acquisition of AstraZeneca by US pharmaceutical giant Pfizer in spring 2014, when the British, despite strong strategic synergies, decided to reject an $117bn takeover bid, due to an insufficient price-offer (Pettypiece, 2014). This essay is going to critically evaluate the concepts of shareholder wealth creation, in light of appropriate evaluation methods for bids and the influence of capital structure. It will be concluded that information asymmetry was one of the core issues in the case, as both parties ultimately misestimated potential synergies. Moreover, it is argued that irrational decisions, made by executive, can significantly impact and eventually destroy shareholder value.

Valuation of Bids

One of the key challenges and, after all, the insurmountable hurdle of the Pfizer-AstraZeneca deal was the agreeing on a takeover price (Pettypiece, 2014). From a shareholder perspective, evaluating the bids for shares is crucial as it is ultimately their risk, savings and value that is affected by a potential merger (Arnold, 2013, p. 366). The literature generally presents market-based, income-based and net-asset (NAV) valuation approaches in this context (Bernstrom, 2014).

Provided that Fama's (1970) Efficient Market Hypotheses holds true and shares constantly reflect the value of a firm, market-based valuations, in terms of market capitalisation, seems to be the most straightforward assessment technique. However, as argued by Malkiel (2003, 2005) and Summers (1986), markets are rarely entirely rational and pricing is therefore often inadequate. In this context the price-earnings ratio (PER), as an advanced evaluation model, includes future market returns (Basu, 1977; Malkiel, 2003). Shareholders can employ the PER in order to estimate the

4

target's total equity value by re-estimating future earnings and multiplying them with benchmark PE-ratios (Sudarsanam, 2010, p. 429). Myers (1984b), however, raises fundamental concerns with the accurate forecasting of future earnings, which, in fact, seemed to be one of the major hurdles in the Pfizer-AstraZeneca case, bearing in mind that long-term estimates are particularly challenging in the pharmaceutical environment (Armstrong & Staley, 2014).

A similar, however, predominantly income-focused approach is the Discounted Cash Flow method (DCF), which Mukherjee, Kiymaz, and Baker (2004) found to be the dominant investment-evaluation approach these days. Essentially detached from the share price, this technique relies on the forecast of post-merger cash flows, discounted to a present value, using the firm's internal rate of return (IRR) (Plenborg, 2002). In addition to the shortcomings of earning forecasts, Myers (1984b) raises concerns about the reliability of estimating a firm's discount rate. Koller, Goedhart, and Wessels (2006) further stress inappropriate perpetuity assumptions to cause misevaluation in the DCF.

A third and entirely different technique is the NAV, which assesses a firm on the fair market value of its assets, less the respective debt obligations (Watson & Head, 2013, p. 323). In contrast to the previous approaches, the NAV ignores future incomes, which, on the one hand makes it more straightforward in its application, however, on the other hand, fails to value intangible assets that are of particular importance for pharmaceutical companies such as Pfizer or AstraZeneca (Boekestein, 2006; Ryan, 2007).

All in all, shareholder can choose from a range of different techniques to assess the appropriate price for the shares they hold. Although it seems as if the approaches partly overcome one another's shortcomings, Bernstrom (2014, p. 16) argues that the overall valuation is effectively unattached from the model utilised, as they all result in similar outcomes. However, Pfizer's executives faced another valuation-issue when arguing that their "final proposal (...) represented [the] full value (...) based on the information that was available" (Pfizer Inc., 2014). Information asymmetry, according to Barney (1988) and Sirower (1997, p. 40), is, in fact, one of the dominant reasons merging parties fail to agree on a takeover price. Differing information in terms of the IRR and potential future incomes may explain the gap between Pfizer's final £55-a-share proposal and AstraZeneca's claim to require an offer higher than £58.85 to recommend it to their shareholders (Ward, 2014b).

Capital Structure

In fact, the IRR, in terms of the weighted average costs of capital (WACC), may have been interpreted fundamentally different by both parties, since Pfizer's CFO D'Amelio proposed gearing, and therefore a change in the average costs of capital (Baxter, 1967), to finance the total takeover bid of $117bn (Armstrong & Staley, 2014). However, the question of whether or not to lever up the balance sheet is highly controversial in the context of shareholder wealth creation.

The modern day capital structure discussion essentially took off with Modigliani and Miller's (1958) irrelevance proposition. Under the assumption of perfect markets, homemade leverage, meaning investors can adapt to any leverage their firm took, increases the owners' equity value (Frank & Goyal, 2007, p. 140; Modigliani & Miller, 1958). Myers (2001) and Miller (1989), however, argue that capital structure decisions do affect shareholders' wealth as a result of costs of imperfections in the market, such as the existence of taxes, agency costs and information asymmetry.

Table 1 Capital Structure Theories that Emerged from Costs of Imperfections

Source: Created by the author, Content as indicated in the Table

Capital Structure Theories	...addresses Modigliani and Miller's (1958) assumption of...	...issuing debt creates shareholder wealth by...
Static Trade-Off (Bradley, Jarrell, & Kim, 1984)	Taxes and Bankruptcy Costs	balancing tax advantages of additional debt against the costs of increasing financial distress
Pecking Order (POT) (Myers, 1984a; Myers & Majluf, 1984)	Information Asymmetry	maximising value of existing shares through borrowing, if internal cash flows are not sufficient to fund capital expenditures
Free Cash Flow (FCF) (Jensen, 1986)	Agency Costs	forcing executives to act in the firm's interest and create cash in order to meet (dangerously high) interest liabilities

6

The traditional view that, up to a point, gearing, in terms of cheaper debt-financing, increases shareholder value can best be described with the Trade-Off theory, which ultimately predicts moderate borrowing across all tax-paying enterprises (MacKie-Mason, 1990; Myers, 2001; Titman, 2002). In this context, Graham (2000), however, found that a large number of firms still operate below their optimal debt-ratio. As this, according to Myers (2001), also holds true for pharmaceutical companies, Pfizer's claim to finance the AstraZeneca deal with outside capital, may be interpreted as a hint that the Americans have not yet reached their optimal capital structure and borrowing would further increase shareholders' wealth.

Myers' POT delivers an explanation for the below-optimum borrowing of enterprises by arguing that companies only take on debt if internal cash flows are not sufficient to fund respective expenditures (Fama & French, 2002; Shyam-Sunder & Myers, 1999). This, in turn, implies that highly levered balance sheets merely reflect a firm's need for external funds, if assumed that executives act in the interest of existing shareholders (Myers, 2001). However, with rating agency Moody's initially expecting Pfizer to use their enormous cash positions, instead of incremental debt, to fund the AstraZeneca deal (Armstrong, 2014), the POT fails to explain D'Amelio's announcement to lever up the balance sheet.

Jensen and Meckling's (1976) found that managers tend to act in their own interest, which not only delivers a second explanation for the below-optimal borrowing of enterprises, but also adds another perspective to the capital structure discussion. According to the FCF-theory, dangerously high debt ratios may add significant value to shareholders as it forces executives to constantly generate and disburse cash (Jensen, 1986).

After all, it can be concluded that companies should be anything but indifferent about their capital structure (Bradley et al., 1984; DeAngelo & Masulis, 1980) and rather strive for an optimal debt ratio that is in-between the two extremes and ultimately maximises shareholders' wealth (Myers, 1984a). Pfizer's claim to raise debt should be considered with caution since the sole purpose may not lie in the creation of shareholder value but in the executives' attempt to not dilute their control in a merged company, following a stock-financed deal (Amihud, Lev, & Travlos, 1990).

Value-Creation in M&As

The method of payment has, in fact, a significant impact on the maximisation of shareholder wealth (Bouwman, Fuller, & Nain, 2003), which poses the question as to whether or not M&As, and the 45%-cash, 55%-share Pfizer-AstraZeneca deal (Armstrong & Staley, 2014) in particular, create value in the first place. Bouwman et al. (2003) present short and long-term stock performances as well as profitability as the three distinct ways to measure the value creation of M&As.

Table 2 Short-Term Impact of M&As on Target and Bidding Company

Source: Created by the author, Content as indicated in the Table

	Target Company	Bidding Company
Successful M&As	• Significant shareholder wealth creation *(Jensen & Ruback, 1983)* • Average 6 to 20% increase on or before announcement date *(Asquith, 1983; Dodd, 1980; Schwert, 1996)* • Stock deals less value than equity deals *(Martynova & Renneboog, 2008)*	• Insignificant shareholder wealth creation *(Jensen & Ruback, 1983)* • Little or no reaction on announcement date *(Asquith, 1983; Dodd, 1980)*
Unsuccessful M&As	• Significant initial shareholder wealth creation *(Jensen & Ruback, 1983)* • Large losses on the announcement of failure *(Asquith, 1983; Dodd, 1980; Ruback, 1988)* • Bidder termination destroy more value than target termination *(Boubakri, Chazi, & Khallaf, 2010; Croci, 2006)*	• No losses on the announcement of failure *(Asquith, 1983; Dodd, 1980; Ruback, 1988)* • Significant losses in-between negotiation process if heading to failure *(Asquith, 1983)*
Value Increasing	*Value Neutral*	*Value Destroying*

In the short-run, defined as the days surrounding the M&A announcement (Asquith, 1983), target and bidding company are expected to create value for their shareholders, although the majority of gains results on the target side (Martynova & Renneboog, 2008). In this context, Asquith (1983) and Ruback (1988) found that the initial value is immediately destroyed when failed negotiations are announced (Target-Shareholder) or predictable (Bidding-Shareholder).

The short-term market reaction in the Pfizer-AstraZeneca case perfectly fits the empirical findings, with AstraZeneca's shares initially rising 14% and eventually crashing 11% during the course of negotiations (BBC News, 2014; Thayer, 2014). Croci (2006), in fact, argues that M&As that have been terminated by the target destroy less value than a bidder-termination. At the same time, Pfizer's shares only marginally adapted to the news; however, experienced a drastic price drop in the interim period, when the failure became foreseeable, which is a characteristic short-term trend in unsuccessful M&A negotiations (Asquith, 1983).

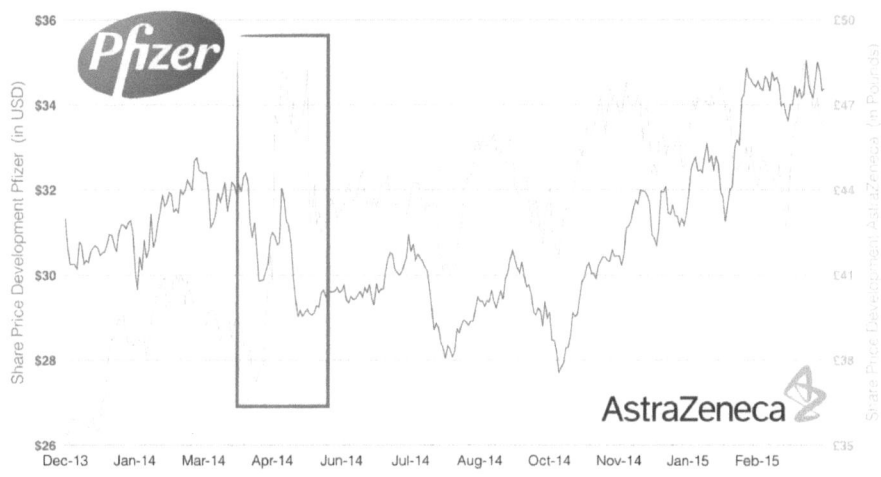

Figure 1 Share Price Development for Pfizer inc. and AstraZeneca plc. (01/12/13 to 30/03/15)

Source: Created by the author, data received from Bloomberg L.P. (2015)

AstraZeneca's shares still trade 25% above before-negotiation-levels (Barbaglia & Sassard, 2014). Schwert (1996) defines this consistent long-term increase in shareholder wealth as *markup* or *premium* that effectively reflects an inefficient market in which owners assume hidden values in their stocks and potentially expect talks to be resumed (Schwert, 2003). By contrast, the fact that Pfizer's shares are currently traded considerably above last year's level may be explained with Jacobsen's (2014) recent findings that shareholders appreciate executives' decisions to withdraw from overpriced deals and thereby extracting private benefits.

Successful M&As, after all, tend to destroy shareholder value in the long-run, in terms of negative abnormal stock performances (Bruner, 2002), meaning stock-prices relative to non-acquiring peers (Bouwman et al., 2003).

Table 3 Long-Term Impact of M&As on Target and Bidding Company

Source: Created by the author, Content as indicated in the Table

	Target Company	Bidding / Combined Company
Successful M&As	*Not Relevant*	• Signifcant negative performance (*e.g. Bruner, 2002*) • Stock deals perform worse than Equity deals (*Loughran & Vijh, 1997; Mitchell & Stafford, 2000*)
Unsuccessful M&As	• Slightly negative long-term performance (*Bradley, Desai, & Kim, 1983; Dodd & Ruback, 1977*) • Indeed significant costs of failure for target firms (*Easterbrook & Jarrell, 1984; Ruback, 1988*)	• Slightly negative performance as a result of negative stock reaction during interim period (*Asquith, 1983*)
Value Increasing	*Value Neutral*	*Value Destroying*

A third, and in the Pfizer-AstraZeneca case not applicable, performance measure is the value creation in terms of increased profits of a combined enterprise (Bouwman et al., 2003). In this context, empiric research, again, confirms that M&As rather destroy than increase shareholder wealth, with Dickerson, Gibson, and Tsakalotos (1997) finding a decrease of return on assets for the bidder-company and Healy, Palepu, and Ruback (1997) reveal only marginal increases in the combined firm's operating cash-flow. In addition, Martynova and Renneboog (2008) found substantial declines in the acquiring firms' share prices, which suggests that anticipated synergies from takeovers are often overstated.

Although it is concluded that M&As rarely create value for shareholders, it can be assumed that businesses will rely on consolidations. For pharmaceutical companies, in particular, M&As are often the only way to overcome so-called pipeline problems, as the acquisition of external technology and patents is expected to secure future sales (Frantz, 2006; Heracleous & Murray, 2001).

Conclusion

The discussion revealed information asymmetry to be the underlying reason for the failure of the Pfizer-AstraZeneca deal. More specifically, the different valuation approaches for the Britons' promising R&D-pipeline (Kanavos & Angelis, 2014) may explain the ultimate price gap. In the end, both shareholder groups seem to appreciate the non-conclusion of the acquisition, as stock prices still trade above earlier levels. From Pfizer's perspective, shareholders seem to treasure that their firm refrained from an acquisition at all costs, as a value increase would have merely been due to tax optimisation, following tax inversions into the UK (Kanavos & Angelis, 2014). In fact, a combined pharma-company of that scale is expected to destroy, or at least not create, shareholder wealth in the long-run (Grabowski & Kyle, 2008).

The negotiations revealed AstraZeneca's key argument of having a superior product pipeline (Bennett & Cortez, 2014). Following a successful acquisition, this value-proposition was, however, expected to be offset by heavy cutbacks in the workforce and R&D-budgets (Kanavos & Angelis, 2014). One can therefore agree with Leif Johansson's statement that a potential deal "would dramatically dilute AstraZeneca shareholders' exposure to [their] unique pipeline" (AstraZeneca plc., 2014). In a wealth maximisation context, the rejection of the deal seems reasonable, given that a smaller, independent and strongly R&D-focussed company can present greater prospects for its shareholders (Chan, Lakonishok, & Sougiannis, 2001; Munos, 2009).

A rather controversial capital structure discussion has led to the conclusion that a more share-based, instead of debt-focussed, financing approach could have increased mutual trust for the deal and, after all, the possibility for it to get through (Bower, 2001). Using borrowed capital to finance projects is, on the one hand, a cheaper source of funding, however, on the other hand, increases the risk for shareholders (Schwartz, 1996). In turn, irrationally acting executives can significantly destroy shareholder wealth by over-leveraging the balance sheet without apparent reasons (Jensen, 1986).

Although the tendency is that the Pfizer-AstraZeneca deal had rather destroyed than created shareholder value, a final assessment would be unreliable at this stage. The concept of shareholder wealth maximisation is highly complex and more of a combination of different attributes on top of the frameworks discussed in this work, such as future dividend pay-outs or executive remuneration (Rappaport, 2006). Nonetheless, it can be concluded that executives, who extract private benefits from business decisions, are not only able to strive for the most efficient debt-ratios but also enhance transparency for shareholders in the valuation of their stocks, which ultimately maximise the overall wealth.

List of References

Amihud, Y., Lev, B., & Travlos, N. G. (1990). Corporate control and the choice of investment financing: The case of corporate acquisitions. *The Journal of Finance, 45*(2), 603-616.

Armstrong, A. (2014, 29 April). Pfizer cash and stock Astrazeneca takeover would be 'credit positive' says Moody's. *The Telegraph*. Retrieved from http://www.telegraph.co.uk/finance/newsbysector/pharmaceuticalsandchemic als/10795333/Pfizer-cash-and-stock-Astrazeneca-takeover-would-be-credit-positive-says-Moodys.html

Armstrong, D., & Staley, O. (2014, 19 May). AstraZeneca Rejects Pfizer $117 Billion Takeover Bid *Bloomberg Business*. Retrieved from http://www.bloomberg.com/news/articles/2014-05-18/pfizer-raises-offer-for-astrazeneca-to-117-billion

Arnold, G. (2013). *Corporate financial management*. Harlow: Pearson.

Asquith, P. (1983). Merger bids, uncertainty, and stockholder returns. *Journal of Financial Economics, 11*(1), 51-83.

AstraZeneca plc. (2014). AstraZeneca Board rejects Pfizer proposal [Press release]. Retrieved from http://www.astrazeneca.com/Media/Press-releases/Article/20140502--astrazeneca-board-rejects-pfizer-proposal

Barbaglia, P., & Sassard, S. (2014, 14 November). AstraZeneca not only game in town for deal-hungry Pfizer. *Reuters*. Retrieved from http://www.reuters.com/article/2014/11/14/us-astrazeneca-m-a-pfizer-idUSKCN0IY1BP20141114

Barney, J. B. (1988). Returns to bidding firms in mergers and acquisitions: Reconsidering the relatedness hypothesis. *Strategic Management Journal, 9*(S1), 71-78.

Basu, S. (1977). Investment performance of common stocks in relation to their price-earnings ratios: A test of the efficient market hypothesis. *The Journal of Finance, 32*(3), 663-682.

Baxter, N. D. (1967). Leverage, Risk of Ruin and The Cost of Capital. *Journal of Finance, 22*(3), 395-403.

BBC News. (2014). AstraZeneca shares soar after Pfizer confirms bid talks. Retrieved 03 May, 2015, from http://www.bbc.co.uk/news/business-27185027

Bennett, S., & Cortez, M. F. (2014, 29 April). AstraZeneca's Soriot Pumped Up the Noise on Drug Pipeline *Bloomberg Business*. Retrieved from http://www.bloomberg.com/news/articles/2014-04-28/astrazeneca-s-soriot-pumped-up-the-noise-on-drug-pipeline#news/articles/2014-04-28/astrazeneca-s-soriot-pumped-up-the-noise-on-drug-pipeline

Bernstrom, S. (2014). *Valuation : The Market Approach* Retrieved from http://northumbria.eblib.com/patron/FullRecord.aspx?p=1680600

Bloomberg L.P. (2015). *Share Price Development for Pfizer inc. and AstraZeneca plc. 01/12/13 to 30/03/15.* Retrieved from: Bloomberg Database

Boekestein, B. (2006). The relation between intellectual capital and intangible assets of pharmaceutical companies. *Journal of Intellectual Capital, 7*(2), 241-253.

Boubakri, N., Chazi, A., & Khallaf, A. (2010). Targets Performance in Terminated Bids: An Empirical Examination. *Quarterly Journal of Finance and Accounting,* 87-111.

Bouwman, C. H. S., Fuller, K., & Nain, A. S. (2003). Stock market valuation and mergers. *MIT SLOAN MANAGEMENT REVIEW, 45*(1), 9-11.

Bower, J. L. (2001). Not All M&As Are Alike—and That Matters. *Harvard Business Review.*

Bradley, M., Desai, A., & Kim, E. H. (1983). The rationale behind interfirm tender offers: Information or synergy? *Journal of Financial Economics, 11*(1), 183-206.

Bradley, M., Jarrell, G. A., & Kim, E. (1984). On the existence of an optimal capital structure: Theory and evidence. *The Journal of Finance, 39*(3), 857-878.

Bruner, R. F. (2002). Does M&A pay? A survey of evidence for the decision-maker. *Journal of Applied Finance, 12*(1), 48-68.

Chan, L. K. C., Lakonishok, J., & Sougiannis, T. (2001). The stock market valuation of research and development expenditures. *The Journal of Finance, 56*(6), 2431-2456.

Croci, E. (2006). Stock price performances of target firms in unsuccessful acquisitions. *Available at SSRN 766304.*

DeAngelo, H., & Masulis, R. W. (1980). Optimal capital structure under corporate and personal taxation. *Journal of Financial Economics, 8*(1), 3-29.

Dickerson, A. P., Gibson, H. D., & Tsakalotos, E. (1997). The impact of acquisitions on company performance: Evidence from a large panel of UK firms. *Oxford Economic Papers, 49*(3), 344-361.

Dodd, P. (1980). Merger proposals, management discretion and stockholder wealth. *Journal of Financial Economics, 8*(2), 105-137.

Dodd, P., & Ruback, R. (1977). Tender offers and stockholder returns: An empirical analysis. *Journal of Financial Economics, 5*(3), 351-373.

Easterbrook, F. H., & Jarrell, G. A. (1984). Do targets gain from defeating tender offers. *NYuL Rev., 59,* 277.

Fama, E. F. (1970). Efficient capital markets: A review of theory and empirical work*. *The Journal of Finance, 25*(2), 383-417.

Fama, E. F., & French, K. R. (2002). Testing trade-off and pecking order predictions about dividends and debt. *Review of financial studies, 15*(1), 1-33.

Frank, M. Z., & Goyal, V. K. (2007). Trade-off and pecking order theories of debt. *Available at SSRN 670543.*

Frantz, S. (2006). Pipeline problems are increasing the urge to merge. *Nature Reviews Drug Discovery, 5*(12), 977-979.

Grabowski, H., & Kyle, M. (2008). Mergers and alliances in pharmaceuticals: effects on innovation and R&D productivity. *The Economics of Corporate Governance and Mergers, 262.*

Graham, J. R. (2000). How big are the tax benefits of debt? *The Journal of Finance, 55*(5), 1901-1941.

Healy, P. M., Palepu, K. G., & Ruback, R. S. (1997). Which takeovers are profitable? Strategic or financial? *Sloan management review, 38*(4), 45-57.

Heracleous, L., & Murray, J. (2001). The urge to merge in the pharmaceutical industry. *European Management Journal, 19*(4), 430-437.

Jacobsen, S. (2014). The death of the deal: Are withdrawn acquisition deals informative of CEO quality? *Journal of Financial Economics, 114*(1), 54-83.

Jensen, M. C. (1986). Agency cost of free cash flow, corporate finance, and takeovers. *Corporate Finance, and Takeovers. American Economic Review, 76*(2).

Jensen, M. C., & Meckling, W. H. (1976). Theory of the firm: Managerial behavior, agency costs and ownership structure. *Journal of Financial Economics, 3*(4), 305-360. doi: http://dx.doi.org/10.1016/0304-405X(76)90026-X

Jensen, M. C., & Ruback, R. S. (1983). The market for corporate control: The scientific evidence. *Journal of Financial Economics, 11*(1–4), 5-50. doi: http://dx.doi.org/10.1016/0304-405X(83)90004-1

Kanavos, P., & Angelis, A. (2014). Acquiring pharmaceutical industry assets in the UK: 1+ 1= 1? *Pharmaceutical medicine, 28*(5), 245-248.

Koller, T., Goedhart, M., & Wessels, D. (2006). Common Errors in DCF Models. Retrieved 01 May, 2015, from http://cdn1.valuewalk.com/wp-content/uploads/2014/07/Common-DCF-Errors_LeggMason.pdf

Loughran, T., & Vijh, A. M. (1997). Do long-term shareholders benefit from corporate acquisitions? *The Journal of Finance, 52*(5), 1765-1790.

MacKie-Mason, J. K. (1990). Do taxes affect corporate financing decisions? *The Journal of Finance, 45*(5), 1471-1493.

Malkiel, B. G. (2003). The efficient market hypothesis and its critics. *Journal of economic perspectives*, 59-82.

Malkiel, B. G. (2005). Reflections on the efficient market hypothesis: 30 years later. *Financial Review, 40*(1), 1-9.

Martynova, M., & Renneboog, L. (2008). A century of corporate takeovers: What have we learned and where do we stand? *Journal of Banking & Finance, 32*(10), 2148-2177.

Miller, M. H. (1989). The Modigliani-Miller Propositions After Thirty Years. *Journal of Applied Corporate Finance, 2*(1), 6-18.

Mitchell, M. L., & Stafford, E. (2000). Managerial decisions and long-term stock price performance. *the Journal of Business, 73*(3), 287-329.

Modigliani, F., & Miller, M. H. (1958). The cost of capital, corporation finance and the theory of investment. *The American economic review*, 261-297.

Mukherjee, T. K., Kiymaz, H., & Baker, H. K. (2004). Merger Motives and Target Valuation: A Survey of Evidence from CFOs. *Journal of Applied Finance, 14*(2), 7-24.

Munos, B. (2009). Lessons from 60 years of pharmaceutical innovation. *Nature Reviews Drug Discovery, 8*(12), 959-968.

Myers, S. C. (1984a). The capital structure puzzle. *The Journal of Finance, 39*(3), 574-592.

Myers, S. C. (1984b). Finance theory and financial strategy. *Interfaces, 14*(1), 126-137.

Myers, S. C. (2001). Capital structure. *Journal of economic perspectives*, 81-102.

Myers, S. C., & Majluf, N. S. (1984). Corporate financing and investment decisions when firms have information that investors do not have. *Journal of Financial Economics, 13*(2), 187-221.

Pettypiece, S. (2014, 11 June). Price the Reason Pfizer-AstraZeneca Deal Died, CFO Says *Bloomberg Business.* Retrieved from http://www.bloomberg.com/news/articles/2014-06-11/pfizer-cfo-says-astrazeneca-deal-broke-down-over-price

Pfizer Inc. (2014). Announcement regarding AstraZeneca Plc. - Statement from Pfizer Inc. [Press release]. Retrieved from http://www.pfizer.com/news/press-release/press-release-detail/announcement_regarding_astrazeneca_plc

Plenborg, T. (2002). Firm valuation: comparing the residual income and discounted cash flow approaches. *Scandinavian Journal of Management, 18*(3), 303-318.

Rappaport, A. (2006). Ten Ways to Create Shareholder Value. *Harvard Business Review, 84*(9), 66--77.

Ruback, R. S. (1988). Do target shareholders lose in unsuccessful control contests? *Corporate takeovers: Causes and consequences* (pp. 137-156): University of Chicago Press.

Ryan, B. (2007). *Corporate finance and valuation*: Cengage Learning EMEA.

Schwartz, A. (1996). A theory of loan priorities. *Corporate Bankruptcy: Economic and Legal Perspectives, 209*, 17.

Schwert, G. W. (1996). Markup pricing in mergers and acquisitions. *Journal of Financial Economics, 41*(2), 153-192.

Schwert, G. W. (2003). Anomalies and market efficiency. *Handbook of the Economics of Finance, 1*, 939-974.

Shyam-Sunder, L., & Myers, S. C. (1999). Testing static tradeoff against pecking order models of capital structure. *Journal of Financial Economics, 51*(2), 219-244.

Sirower, M. L. (1997). *The synergy trap: How companies lose the acquisition game*: Simon and Schuster.

Sudarsanam, P. S. (2010). Creating value from mergers and acquisitions: the challenges. Harlow: Financial Times Prentice Hall.

Summers, L. H. (1986). Does the stock market rationally reflect fundamental values? *The Journal of Finance, 41*(3), 591-601.

Thayer, A. M. (2014, 26 May). AstraZeneca Rejects Pfizer's Final Offer. *Chemical & Engineering News.* Retrieved from http://cen.acs.org/articles/92/i21/AstraZeneca-Rejects-Pfizers-Final-Offer.html

Titman, S. (2002). The Modigliani and Miller theorem and the integration of financial markets. *Financial management*, 101-115.

Ward, A. (2014a, 26 December). Big pharma cashes in as M&A fever sweeps sector. *Financial Times*. Retrieved from http://www.ft.com/cms/s/0/f742b876-8aa3-11e4-8e24-00144feabdc0.html#axzz3YhGABKvO

Ward, A. (2014b, 26 May). Pfizer admits defeat in AstraZeneca bid. *Financial Times*. Retrieved from http://www.ft.com/cms/s/0/418ce3cc-e4b7-11e3-9b2b-00144feabdc0.html#axzz3YufTwMb3

Watson, D., & Head, A. (2013). *Corporate finance: principles and practice*. Harlow: Pearson.

YOUR KNOWLEDGE HAS VALUE